T0067964

and She rose too

RENNY

author HOUSE

AuthorHouse™
1663 Liberty Drive
Bloomington, IN 47403
www.authorhouse.com
Phone: 833-262-8899

Published by AuthorHouse 10/27/2021

ISBN: 978-1-6655-4263-0 (sc)
ISBN: 978-1-6655-4262-3 (e)

Print information available on the last page.

Table of Contents

Reflection

Voyage

today i take my first trip alone
the only emotion i feel is excitement
this feeling of independence
is a little overwhelming but settling
my getaway may not be far
but i still get away
i finally get to fly free
just me
no restrictions
no deadlines
no hassle
no anxiety
so thank you
to everyone who let me go
in the process of helping me grow
as a breath of fresh air
awaits

Necessity

tell them i was
the dead leaves
that boosted
you're wildfire

Renny

my dark days are my most open and vulnerable days
my mind goes crazy over the little things that won't
matter a week from now
my heart sheds tears for the insecure moments
the truth is always harder to swallow during this time
and no one is deemed comforting
the silent screams and shallow cries come through
louder than before
it's only a matter of time till i get lost in the whirlpool
of my thoughts
bursts of anger erupt too often
it becomes unnoticeable to my eye
the same hurt i'm drowning in
i impose on another 10x harder
it's the sick cycle of suffocating in a bad dream
waking up in a cold sweat
to only realize you're still sleeping
these dark days feel the longest
i wished someone will come save me
but i'm distant and unreachable
these dark days are shittiest
yet somehow i grow stronger

have you ever started a song
and halfway through
you just get so lost in your thoughts
you don't notice the music in the
background
until it slowly fades back in

now replace the music with a person
the people that treat us like shit
or don't value us as a human
we usually treat them the same way

we get so wrapped into
all the good parts of them
the soft sweet talking
we turn a blind eye to the bad
we choose to let them go
but only for a short while
until we slowly let them back in

and the cycle repeats itself
almost unconsciously
as if it has turned into
a routine
to love the ones who hurt us
to settle and accept a love
that's beneath us
but why?

Youngest of Five

i was born the youngest of five
but i was raised an only child
my siblings are still in my life but
not as close as i'd wish to be
i love them dearly
they mean the world to me
and their always there for me when shit hits the fan
but i don't want to be the odd man out anymore
i wanna bond and get to know them
not just see them at family gatherings and when they
come over once and a while
i wanna call them and just talk and be comfortable
doing so
get advice talk about the struggles in my life and
theirs
i want to truly feel like their little sister
at all times

Renny

#daddyissues

hey dad
i'm 20yrs old now
you've missed 20yrs of my life
i'm smart, determined and outgoing
you'd be hella proud of me
but where were you during all that time
just a figment of my imagination
i wonder at all do you think about my mother
and if she had me?
do you wonder where she is or what she's doing?
or maybe where am i and what i'm doing?
you've been on my mind heavy
this christmas season
maybe it's mutual and you feel just i as do
as if something is missing.
i'm here if you're looking for me
i'm ready to be found

I Woke Up With Pregnancy on My Mind   05/10/19

i woke up with pregnancy on my mind
the thought of carrying my child for about 10 months
excites me
the glow
the swollen feet
the cravings

i woke up with pregnancy on my mind
my stomach stretching itself
to make room for my angel
giving him or her the space he or she
needs to develop
to grow
to manifest

i woke up with pregnancy on my mind
my craving for ice chips will be my indicator
that i'm not living for just myself anymore
for those 10 months & beyond
i'll nurture you till you decide to join us
in the world

Renny

i woke up with pregnancy on my mind
we'll listen to solange in nature
meditate to put you at ease
we'll dance to sango while i cook us
something good to eat
we'll jam to popcaan in the shower

i woke up with pregnancy on my mind
we'll read so many black authors
poetry will be your middle name
i loved you before i knew you
and i'm going to love you even more
when i met you forever

i woke up with pregnancy on my mind
the thought of you is joyous
uplifting
i promise to give you my all
even when you cause me morning sickness
give me back pain
force me to only sleep on my side
i promise to be slow to anger with you
i promise to listen to first and ask questions later

i woke up with pregnancy on my mind
no matter what you put my physical body through
my love for you will never
cease
wander
or
fade
i woke up with pregnancy on my mind

Renny

Fears

who do you call when fear
has shown up to your house unannounced?

it didn't knock just barged right it
ignorant to the situation at hand
only worried about itself

the level of disrespect fear holds
is astronomical
it does what it wants
when it wants
no questions asked

it holds you hostage
makes you a prisoner within your own mind
takes you for ransom but never gets
the pay out

fear likes being in control
it likes knowing
it can keep you in check
likes to push your buttons
then play victim

fear enjoys watching you
second guess yourself
it sees joy in having you feel
unworthy

scared
shallow
lost

fear is the greatest conman
mastermind of head games
trickiest trickster
there ever was

Renny

Darker Days

there are times i wish i didn't exist
because no one seems to
appreciate me being here
i'm more of a burden
i cause more pain than joy
so why do i still wake each morning
trying to thrive to prove to those
that don't like me
the reason they should
it never works
and i'm always lead back
to my dark twisted fantasy

Childhood is Pure

childhood is pure
innocent
unknowing of serious dangerous
your family will do absolutely anything to protect
and make sure you never get robbed of it
during childhood how do you tell the
difference between being overprotective
and infatuation
the saying goes stranger danger
but what's the saying when the danger isn't a stranger
better yet this person was there for all your childhood
mistakes, birthdays
this person is here to protect you
and show you guidance
when the guidance become an invasion
that gut feeling tells you something isn't right but
they say
it's okay
it's fine
don't tell anybody
they won't get it
it's our game
let's keep this our little secret
truth of that gut feeling starts to settle
you begin to become one with the little secret

the reflection in the mirror gets harder to bare and
the showers just don't seem to be hot enough to melt
away the damaged
the used layer of skin
he's the only one who had fun with this game
this little secret we wouldn't dare to share
was too shameful
for the ears of elders and too infectious for the young
you hated the day you were caught but not as much as
did when i actually spoke those words
i let the letters form and my voice heard
you raped me
that was a burden i held on to for far too long
my young shoulders couldn't bare the weight anymore
having to put on a happy face seeing you every family
gathering
while deep down part of me cries loudly
you have took away my childhood
and that's okay
i bend
but i don't break
you've made me strong
resilient
empowered

Heartache

Do You Notice Me?　　　7/13/18

do you notice me?
the way i stare at you oh so lovingly
how i go out of my way to make sure you're happy
the way i push myself off the edge in hopes of you
catching me
pretending to not care when you tell me about other
women you've dealt with
my hair is cut differently, did you see?
did you notice that i give you all of me
looking for your validation to some degree

did you notice that i love you?
through all the pain i never put anyone above you
i stayed true
to you
i acted stupidly before
but now more than ever i just want you
i want you to notice the growth in me
the healthy life choices
personal goals i set and accomplished
how i've changed for the better
now more than ever we'll be so good together

i want you to notice me
but not just me
you with me
what we could do

what we could be
turn that we into us again
and do everything we dreamed

i notice you
with all your dreams and hopes
the goals you set and met
how determined you are to strive
your willingness to always turn a blind eye
how people judge your seriousness as you being mean
but it's just a defense because you're scared to let
people in
the way you enjoy the rain as if it's gods gift just
for you
the way your eyes light up in the calmness of your
excitement
how you caress my face and kiss my forehead ever so
gently
the way you say my name with such grace as if it was
crafted for your lips

but i don't think you notice me
the way i notice me
the way i notice you
the way i notice us
and all that we could be

so ill ask you again
and tell me truthfully
do you notice me?

i don't want to be your one night stand at 2am
i don't want you to only hit me up between the hours
11-7
you don't want me
you don't want to get to know me
see how i'm doing
i refuse to be someone's booty call
my pussys great i know
but maybe if you spend a little more time looking into
my soul and not through it
you'd see that i'm pretty great too

Temporary Forevers   07/27/18

temporary forevers
they may not last too long
but just enough to have a good time
just enough to feel the buzz

In Love with Love   05/29/18

being in love with love
is a blessing and a curse
you know exactly what you want and how you want it
but the truth is not everyone is built to the standards
you set for your ideal love
so you lower the standards and adapt
you disregard your love for holding hands, pda, love
letters, stolen glances
they implement their idea of love onto you
you convince yourself that their
your soul mate
being in love with love sets you up for failure in
relationships
you imagine movie scene scenarios
that aren't likely in real life
you get so wrapped up in scene of what if
you lose touch with reality

Letter to the Side Chick 11/05/17

dear you,
i know he confides in you
so tell me what you do that i don't
help me spice it up
is it truly me or is it him?
does he hold tight when you have missionary sex
that real close intimacy?
does he whisper in your ear sweet nothings that send
chills through your bones?
does he let you cum first and express how beautiful
you are after?
does he kiss you slowly with just enough pressure to
make you melt into his soul?
tell how he makes you feel
i don't hate you and i'm not mad
i just wanna get to know him through your eyes

Renny

How Do You Separate Love and Complacency?   08/22/19

once a bond is built
there's not much you can say about it
that's going to turn me off
instead i'll turn on you and continue
to stick beside it
routines develop quickly
as the bond strengthens overtime
feelings of excitement, giddy, overwhelming joy
fade into dull, organized, stale boredom
the love that once was
is it gone?
or was it there to begin with?
from the start it was the perfect set up
complacency happens as we do the same
thing every time we see each other
fights over the same topics
there's no growth
no healing
but there's lot of manipulation
condescending tendencies flourish
that "i love you" once held so much meaning
only gets used as a band aid now
pacify the heartbreak and the sadness

in the good times there will be bad times
good times are short lived
bad times last forever
it seems the lines between love and complacency
merge to one lane and there's no exit
no destination in route
just a long road ahead

Letter to The Wife   11/21/18

dear mrs,
i understand how you're feeling
because i was in that same place
the unknown
lost for words
there's no confusion
i posses no interest in him
i only want the sex
it's pretty good
it's actually really amazing
he doesn't make love to me
but i don't want that
it's rough
coarse
very non romantic
he's dominate
but i love it
it's refreshing and new
vibrant yet raw
you wouldn't understand
because it's not meant for you
how we do what we do
is our story
i respect you as a woman but mrs.
the man you love
is worst individual
i've ever met in my life

Craving Intimacy   11/21/18

currently craving intimacy
the soft touch of another
sweet whispers in my ear
warm embrace

as our body heat transfer
into each other's soul
running your fingers
down the slope of my back
heartbeat slows down
so slow it feels nonexistent

our breathing synchronize
inhale the cold dispassion
exhale anew vibration
you tell me you love me
without words

your eyes
with every look, deep longing stare
dilated pupils speak volumes
so high off your touch

Renny

the softness of your voice
cradles me like a newborn baby
tender kisses that land on my forehead
my cheeks the nape of my neck
we fall into each other hopeless
completely unguarded
selfless without end

The Play

act I

it started with art and an awkward glance for far too
long
you explained to me your friends art
it was the introduction

act II

location: the after party
the glances started again with slight warm nervous
smiles
commence the drinking
sip after sip the easier it was
to finally get the guts to say wassup

act III

the plot thickens in act III when you started telling
me about you, intrigued i was drawn to you like i've
known you for years

with our never ending eye contact
and my quick lesson on how to give / receive compliments
the excitement grew between us

Renny

act IV

our kiss was short but sweet
we teased each other until it became
unbearable
the bathroom was our safe heaven

you fucked my body
in the most elegant fashion
and still made sure that i came before you did.

thank you north carolina

in a world where women are silenced
for being mistreated
told they shouldn't dress a certain way
in order to not attract unwanted attention
seen in no other fashion than an object
just another body
for men to use and abuse
as they please
women are looked at as second class citizens
our feelings are not deemed worthy
therefore our truths hold no real value
no substance to the male reader
we're told to give a man what he wants
do as we're told
don't talk back
be housewives
cook
clean
bare children
we can't be smarter or have a better job
in fear of hurting his pride
don't want to make him feel inferior
because after all
men are superior
right?

does me telling you exactly what i want
and how i want it make you uncomfortable ?
i just wanted to have sex and be really good friends
but you just asked why?
why complicate things with feelings
when we don't have to
now that i told you what i want
will you deliver?
if not, that's fine there's plenty of fish in the sea

viewing you in this light is scary
but if something doesn't scare you is it worth doing?
it's risky asf
i'm learning to take risk
trust my intuition
my intuition keeps rooting for you
let's hope you don't let her down

Renny

Takers

i am a cookie jar
full of delicious cookies
your favorites
your wants
your needs

you open me up and take what serves you
every second
minute
hour
day
week
month
year

you never fill me back up
but you continue to take
take
take
take

til one day you decide
you don't need me anymore
i don't have what you need
want
or desire

you exchange me
with a new cookie jar
but you're never satisfied
taking is in your dna
it's what you do

you'll always follow your ritual of
exchanging and acquiring new cookies jars
because it serves you
only you

Renny

Intimacy

come into me
and see what nobody else gets to see
but are you deemed worthy?
how do i know that you aren't a messenger pigeon,
with installed cheat codes that leave me smitten?
don't grab the key to unlock my vault
if in the end all you're going to do is bolt

my heart is big
big enough for the two of us
but it's fragile
and easily broken
hold it close to you
showcase it as a token
never let it
drop
shatter
or chip
because its recovery will be a
grueling bitch of a trip

so if and when we become intimate
be aware my heart won't rest a minute
with fear of your false pretenses
when your true bird intentions arrive
you'll tell them how i
was the greatest tree
you ever built your nest in

Renny

your eyes capture the essence of a room
it showcases your beauty without a spoken word
utterly and completely breathtaking
the way you look at me
with those looking eyes
the soft smile they give
when i catch you looking at me
what's that called?
smeyes
you say a lot by just one glance
truth be told
i'm loving the story their sharing with me

Mask

you were different
finally my dream man is here
holding my hands, kissing my forehead
he is tangible
he makes me giggle and blush
you opened your heart to me and i to you
forever we engrained ourselves together
for lifetimes to come

relationships have their ups and down
that's expected i didn't fret
i always showed my hand
wearing my heart on sleeve
i kept up with date night, made dinner,
all the wifey duties

i picked up when you fell short
in hopes that you'd be able to
pick yourself up again

silly me
i should have believed you when you showed me
who you were the first time
you survive by using others for your advantage
with no consideration of the damage

Renny

you never offer a hand but always have your hand out
you cheat, steal and lie your way through
something
anything
everything

i painted pretty pictures of our family
to hide the truth of our home life
i was raising a husband
instead of having a husband
i was protecting a man
that would never do the same

i am no longer your doormat
i am no longer your slave
i am no longer your atm
i am no longer your safety net
i am no longer your wife
i am no longer a well you can pull water from
i am no longer your life line
i am no longer the mother you wished you had
i am done hiding behind a mask

Awakening

Hurt

the truth hurts but not as much
as long as the lies you tell to hide it

let's stop telling women to teach their daughters
to be less provocative
less outspoken
less hardworking
less driven
less sexy
less powerful
instead
let's change the conversation
let's tell men to teach their sons to be
more respectful
more open minded
more caring
more in tune with their emotions
more consensual
less afraid of powerful women
more conscious of what they say
more supportive
less predatory
simple changes can make the biggest impacts

Falling in Love

the next time i fall in love
i want it to be breathtaking
all consuming
elaborate
secure
genuine
eloquent
one of a kind
exciting
deeply rooted
so amazingly refreshing
that either one of us
gets tired or jaded by it
instead we just live
in each and every
moment we share together
as if it was our last
noticing all the idiosyncrasies
the flaws
hot tempered
slick mouthed
bad attitude
petty behavior
and still looking into each
others eyes and seeing all the good

in one another completely
wholeheartedly accepting
each other for
who we are now
who we used to be
who we want to be
unconditional
extremely comfortable
a love so strong
you look at each other and feel
at home
a sense of safety
security
honesty

Strong Willed   11/21/18

in hopes of gaining strength
i slip on the resistance bands
and push forward
the person holding me back
and encouraging me to go
is me

Brighter Side

trust is something i give away but never gets returned
having faith that everyone is as nice as they seem
some might call it naive
i just call it believing in the greater good
the world may suck but it can't be as bad as they make
it out to be
look forward to the possibility
of positive endings
there's always a reason
and where there's a reason
there's a silver lining
live happily ever after
in the silver lining

Black Women's Beauty   03/30/18

there's nothing more beautiful than a black woman
being unapologetically black
coconut oiled nourished skin
just glistening in the slightest touch of light, her kinky
curly spiral hair just
sitting on her head proudly
her crown flourishing
elegantly
peacefully
her natural beauty shines through any distress or
discomfort she may be facing
her soul is the purest of pure gold
sometimes it's too much for one to handle
but her chin stays up and her head is held high, no one
fights for truth honesty and compassion like her
her will to persevere is underrated
her motivation to keep going
to strive, ambition through the roof
the taste she leaves on your tastebuds is undeniably
sweet
it should come with a caution sign
her sly confidence mixed with her fierce attitude
will always end in an astonished standing ovation.
she carries the world on her back
has the strength of a thousand men

but yet never really complains until she's fed up with
the disrespect of being treated like a doormat
so she roars louder than any lion
and truth be told she's heard across every nation
the silent hush amongst the trees
knowing she's heard and reciprocated through the
breeze

Renny

Revelations

when a friendship or relationship ends
you shouldn't bury that loss
rather than praise it
celebrate it
with loving arms
embrace the growth
that's about to happen to you
you're going to break in the beginning
but once you blossom
there's no stopping your urge
to show your face to the sun
you're vision is so tunneled
nothing can blindside you
in the midst of your growth
you find the beauty in everything
that once was
that is
and that will be

Do You

in a world where shame and judgement is made first
and asking questions or being understanding comes
last
i say do what you love to do
not because you have to
but because you need to
because it's who you really are
you gotta be true with yourself
in every aspect
and once that is embedded
in your brain
your truth is gonna be hella radiant
it'll blind the ones who don't get you
while empowering the ones who do

Renny

In Our Lifetime   07/28/19

in our lifetime
are we only subjected to one true love?
or
is it multiple
with each love there's a new experience
how do you know when you've met "the one"
how does it feel?
maybe finding" the one"
is old out dated a norm that's not so normal any-
more
we gravitate to what feels good even though we know
there's something that feels better
in this age
maybe it's easier to find anew after something
comforting fades
could love be a spectrum?
can i love two people romantically at the same time?
or can the heart only take it one by one

Trauma Response

we don't really deal with trauma
we mask it
we search for distractions
we lust for temporary forevers
but when it comes to facing it head on
we turn into deer
who's blinded by headlights
lost in the pain
the drama
the chaos that is within you
it shows up during outbursts
of anger
waves
of depression
stress
from the mania
they say being vulnerable is a weakness
a trait for the unfit
but some burdens take two to carry
once you're willing to stop carrying it alone

Renny

Strength

you are a lot stronger than you think you are
you've been through things that no one should ever
i mean ever have to go through
yet you remained resilient
you fought each battle
and won with an army of one
you continuously bounce back

with every new downfall
the latest installment of the world vs you
the eagerness to fight isn't the problem
you don't mind the fight
you surely put up a good one

it's reaching the halfway mark
when your arms start getting tired
shortness of breath
feeling a bit winded
lightheaded

the inner conflict with yourself begins
it keeps you restless
on edge a little nervous
that's when it happens

that unknown fear of losing creeps in
despite everything that you've overcome prior
the doubts
the unanswered questions
the lack of support
the nonstop feeling of inadequacy

everything is heavy
feelings of uncertainty hold you captive

is it worth it in the end?
will it make a difference?
what's the point?
i'll just give up.

but you power through
graceful and effortless
to the blind eye
to the knowing spectator
you arise a true warrior

Silence

there's a moment in the dark
when things get still, quiet
all is peaceful

the mind shuts off
the body begins to relax
the tears melt away
the heart beats slower
the breath is long and drawn out

there's this moment
a moment of nothingness
where nothing hurts
truths aren't painful
sadness fades

temporary happiness comes in
for the moment
there's safety, comfort
the silence brings healing
it brings self awareness

in the silence
you become alive
in the silence
you start the rebirth

New Beginnings Pledge   10/01/21

here's to new friends
new experiences
different places
and the start of beautiful memories
i, *enter name here* declare to live my life to the
fullest
to live my best life
as headass
as reckless
as unquestionably pleasing
than i ever have before
any negative energy brought to me shall not prosper
i will be a radiantly alluring magnetic queen

Renny

Printed in the United States
by Baker & Taylor Publisher Services